Scroll Saw Portraits

by Gary Browning

Fox
Chapel Publishing

1970 Broad Street • East Petersburg, PA 17520
www.FoxChapelPublishing.com

The first edition of *Scroll Saw Portraits* was first published in 2001 by Fox Chapel Publishing Company, Inc. This second edition includes a revised and expanded step-by-step demonstration on making a pattern from a photograph, expanded pattern-mounting instructions and 20 new patterns.

Publisher: Alan Giagnocavo
Book Editor: Ayleen Stellhorn
Editorial Assistant: Gretchen Bacon
Desktop Specialist: Linda L. Eberly, Eberly Designs Inc.

ISBN-13: 978–1–56523–251–8
ISBN-10: 1–56523–251–8
Library of Congress Control Number: 2004102186

To learn more about the other great books from Fox Chapel Publishing, or to find a retailer near you, call toll-free 1-800-457-9112 or visit us at **www.FoxChapelPublishing.com**.

Note to Authors: We are always looking for talented authors to write new books in our area of woodworking, design, and related crafts. Please send a brief letter describing your idea to Peg Couch, Acquisition Editor, 1970 Broad Street, East Petersburg, PA 17520.

Printed in China
10 9 8 7 6 5 4 3 2

FOREWORD

by Alan Giagnocavo
Publisher, *Scroll Saw Workshop* Magazine

When one tries to conjure up the words to describe Gary Browning, the Latin motto Semper Fi comes quickly to mind: in life, in word and in his craft, he's always faithful. Thanks to his Marine Corps-bred determination to follow through, adapt and overcome, Gary has converted his woodworking talents into scroll saw portraits and pattern presentations that are indeed "picture perfect."

Gary was born in Cumberland, Maryland, in 1970. He graduated from Boonsboro High School in 1989. While in school Gary's studies were supplemented by a steady diet of track and field, which included cross country running, pole vaulting and burning up all his one- and two-mile relay races. What's more, sometimes he vaulted and ran three races in a single meet.

Early on in his high school days, Gary's athletic prowess earned him the nickname "Sarge" from his coaches and teammates. They all knew that this fast-footed teen was Armed Forces bound. True to their predictions, seven days after high school Gary boarded a Greyhound to Parris Island, South Carolina. His journey to become a United States Marine had begun.

In the Corp, Browning was a rifleman and marksmanship instructor. Two of his most memorable moments were walking off the parade deck in boot camp as a Marine to shake the hand of his father, a former Marine, and coming home after the Desert Storm War. For Gary, becoming a Marine was more than taking that leap into manhood: it was having that overpowering sense of joy that a son shares by walking, literally, in his father's footsteps. He left the Marine Corps with an Honorable Discharge, several distinguished service medals and, you guessed it . . . the rank of Sergeant.

Life after the Marines is filled with memories of having just enough money for the deposit and first month's rent on a small apartment. But soon he found employment installing alarms and fire systems, a trade he still enjoys today. Life continued to bless him with a beautiful wife and two sons, Robert and Chase—Gary's pride, joy and inspiration.

Gary, who admits to having some artistic ability, got into scroll sawing primarily because photographs of his immediate family members were scarce. Whether it's scrolling the Duke, Marilyn Monroe, Dorothy or Geronimo, Gary has a keen eye and passion for discerning shadows, prominent expressions, subtle facial features and curves. His scroll-work, furthermore, aptly captures its subjects with flowing lines that cannot be duplicated via the camera's lens alone.

This book captures all the lessons that Gary has learned since the first time he fired up a scroll saw and tried to create a portrait. It's Gary's wish that the following pages will ease your journey to realizing the joy that portrait scrolling brings.

TABLE OF CONTENTS

TABLE OF CONTENTS

I designed this book to aid you in using a scroll saw to create a personalized reflection of a person, animal or object in wood. My hope is that you will practice the techniques presented here and then make your own Scroll Saw Portraits from photographs in your own family photo albums.

The process is not as complex as some of the artwork may look. Any photograph can be made into an easy, intermediate or difficult pattern, depending on your skill level. I will start by showing you how to generate a workable pattern from a favorite photograph or drawing, then guide you through cutting, finishing and framing.

The methods that I outline here are gained from my own experience, and I believe they can be easily adapted to anyone's style or technique. Scrolling is a great passion of mine, as well as a relaxing outlet. I am only too happy to share my knowledge to further interest you in this wonderful and easy to learn hobby.

Enjoy!
Gary Browning

Editor's Note: Gary Browning maintains a small website to share his artwork and patterns with other scrollers.

You can visit his site at *www.angelfire.com/md2/creativewood/browning.htm.*

DEDICATION

To My Mother Mary and My Brother Robert—whom I miss very much. I'm doing my best to make you both proud.

GALLERY

SCROLL SAW PORTRAITS

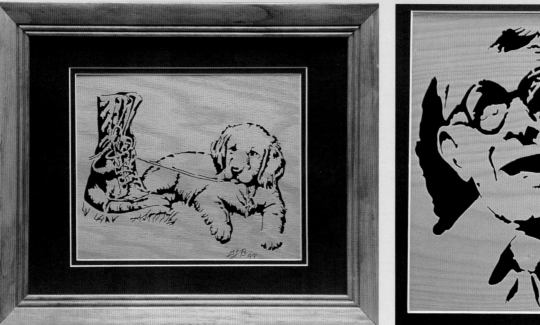

SCROLL SAW PORTRAITS

Scroll Saw Portraits

Scroll Saw Portraits

GALLERY

MAKING PORTRAIT PATTERNS

My scroll saw portrait techniques expand on the basic idea of the silhouette. The silhouette was made long ago as a means of profiling an individual's outline. It was also a form of paper cutting that is still practiced today. Typically, the subject of a silhouette picture is created in a black-colored medium, whether it be ink or paper.

That black shape is then mounted on a white or lighter colored background.

With today's technology, an artist can generate much more detail than the traditional paper or ink silhouettes. Details that show the wrinkles in the face, the position of the eyes and the lines of the ear can be added to make the silhouette more lifelike. I make the majority of my scroll-sawed portraits from existing photographs.

My technique is to scroll the silhouetted image of a person or an animal in light-colored wood. The actual image of the person is removed and the remaining piece of wood is mounted on a black background. The subject's silhouette now shows in black and is very distinct against the light colored wood.

Choosing the Best Pictures

Most people, when they see a moment in time that they want to capture forever, take a picture of that moment. Those photographs are then kept in a family photo album or framed and hung on a wall. These photos often tell the good stories of our lives. We may have photographs of the wedding of a dear friend or pictures of a child's birthday party. Perhaps you have a photograph of a beloved family dog chewing on a bone or of a cat sleeping contentedly in a window. Many photo albums are filled with landscape and scenery pictures from family vacations or quiet get-aways. Each of these photos holds a memory—and each can be transformed into a scroll-sawed keepsake.

Why turn a photo into a wooden picture? First,

scrollers are always looking for something unique to scroll. I can just about guarantee you'll find the most unique patterns right there in your own photo album. And second, the nostalgia involved makes a scrolled photograph something to treasure. Your handiwork will no doubt be on permanent, prominent display.

One man gave me a photo of himself and his wife during World War II in Germany. It was an old black and white photo. It was in excellent condition and in focus. He wanted me to make a likeness of his wife because she had just passed away recently. I treated that photo like it was a one-thousand-dollar bill because I didn't want to harm it in any way. The piece turned out excellent, and my customer was very happy. These types of photographs make the best projects because the finished pieces really touch the person

who receives them.

Photos are also the best and easiest way to convert what you see into a workable pattern. Most of the pattern-making work is already done for you. There is no need to draw (or in my case, draw, erase and re-draw) the subject. You also don't need to cajole your subject into sitting still for long periods of time. My six-year-old does a lot of cute things, but I'm just not fast enough to draw it before he moves on to the next activity. A photograph can capture everything literally in the blink of an eye.

The most important thing to consider when choosing a photograph for a pattern is focus. A lot of detail is lost during the transfer from the photograph to the wood, and if the photo is out of focus, your pattern will lose even more detail. The second most important thing to consider is quality. It is best to have as many photos of the subject as you can so you have a wide variety of pictures from which to choose.

As an example, look at one of the photographs in your wallet. Perhaps you have a picture in there of your wife or your granddaughter or someone else you

hold dear. If your wallet pictures are like mine, they are worn and the edges are torn from years of carrying them around and showing them off. Could you make a good portrait pattern from just that photo? Or would it help to have another picture? You can get better detail from a close-up of a boy on a bicycle than from a small wallet-sized school picture. If the subject is small in scale and standing in the middle of the field, you will not see enough detail in the face when you crop and enlarge the head and bust area. When the photo is close up, all of the small features are present for you to work with.

If you are taking the pictures yourself, take several crisp pictures in different levels of light. If the subject is dark, it is a good practice to apply a lot of light. If the subject is light in color, less light is better. The highlights and shadows in the photo must be crisp. Details will be easier to see, and you'll end up with a much better pattern.

When you are taking your own photographs, remember that more is always better, especially when you are working with children or animals. As an example, I took my own photos to make a scrolled portrait of my uncle's English bulldog. Of the 20 pictures I took, only two were useable for the pattern-making process.

Try to choose pictures with a solid background color, if possible. Solid backgrounds are easier to delete when you make a pattern from the photo. Solid backgrounds may not always be possible, especially on candid photographs. A "noisy" background doesn't make the photo unusable, it just makes the pattern-making process more time consuming.

If you are making a pattern of a person, try to find

a close-up photograph of his or her face. You may even want to take some additional pictures yourself. Photograph the subject from the chest up. The closer you get with the camera, the more detail you will have for your pattern. If you wish to incorporate the background, remember to keep the main focus of the shot on the person; they are the most important aspect of the piece you are creating.

I recently made a scrolled portrait that featured three of my relatives. I used their old school pictures and made three separate patterns. Then I traced each pattern individually to the same piece of wood. This technique is a real time saver and will help you get the end result you want without a lot of trial and error.

Above all, as you search for photographs to convert to portraits, don't get discouraged. Making a scrolled portrait is a challenge, especially if you have never attempted something like this before. My best advice is to start out with a picture of a person's face; save the background and any props for later. Just like

learning to ride a bike, scroll-sawed portraits will become easier as you spend more time scrolling. Take small steps, and remember that the end result will be a warm, heartfelt smile as a thank you for a magnificent gift.

WHAT TO LOOK FOR: PHOTO CHECKLIST

Look through your family photo album for photos with the following traits. These pictures will make the best scrollsaw portrait patterns.

✔ in focus
✔ subject not torn or faded
✔ solid background
✔ good highlights
✔ good shadows
✔ lots of close-up detail

Lesser quality photos can be used, but making patterns from them will require some extra time and effort.

Converting the Photo

Converting the subject in the photograph to a workable portrait pattern is often the hardest part of a project. Your goal is to take the subject's likeness and turn it into a common black-and-white pattern.

You aren't looking for shades of gray; just plain black ink on plain white paper. The black areas of the pattern will be cut away from the wood, and the white paper is the wood that remains to form the silhouette.

Again, don't get discouraged. It takes some time and some practice to be able to look at a photograph and translate it into a silhouette image.

Drawing Freehand

If you or someone you know has enough talent to draw a good likeness of the subject in the photograph, you may want to go the traditional pattern-making route. This method requires drawing the subject freehand in pencil, ink or charcoal. Start with the basic outline of the subject. (Fig. A) Then add all of the inside detail that shows the subject's character. This includes the eyes, the shape of the nose, the mouth, and smile lines, any waves in the hair, etc. (Fig. B) After the drawing is complete, go back over the drawing, filling some of the white areas until the drawing looks like a film negative. (Fig. C) Remember that the black coloring cannot close off the white areas completely. (Fig. D) If the white area is closed off, the wood will not be supported in any way and your design will fall apart when you scroll it.

Freehand Illustration

Fig. A – Draw the basic outline of the subject in black on white paper.

Fig. B – Add in the details of the subject's face.

Fig. C – Color in the drawing until it resembles a negative.

PART ONE

Tracing

Tracing is an option for those who are not confident in their abilities to draw. Simply trace the photograph onto tracing paper to create a pattern. You can combine elements from several photographs by tracing the elements from each photo onto one piece of tracing paper. Be sure to use a pencil and a light touch so you don't damage the photo.

Computer–Aided Design

The computer has had the most profound influence on the advancement of pattern-making, especially for me. Not everyone, myself included, can draw like a pro, but most can point and click. If you're new to computers, visit your local office supply store or check the yellow pages for authorized computer dealers. With the cost of computers today, the machine is really worth the price for all that it can accomplish.

The computer itself is very important, but the software running on the computer is just as important. If you buy a car without tires, you will not get very far. The same goes with computers and software. There are so many software titles out there, and just about everyone of them will aid you in making patterns. Several titles you will want to review include Adobe Photoshop, Corel Draw, Photo Draw 2000, and Paint Shop Pro. Also review freeware and shareware programs on the Internet.

You'll also need a scanner or a digital camera to get the photograph into the computer. Flatbed scanners are very reasonable in cost now, and most will scan photos in black-and-white or color, so you can use them for purposes other than pattern-making. Digital cameras are priced competitively low and offer quick capture and retrieval of images. Review your options carefully with a salesman who is familiar with the equipment. You may want to stay with a traditional camera and have your photos developed by a film processor before scanning them into the computer.

Plan to spend some time becoming familiar with the software program and the scanner that you purchase. Manuals are not always easy to follow, but there are many books published now that explain the software's functions in clearer terms. Your local school district or library may offer classes on using computers and illustration software. The more time you spend learning how to run the programs, the less frustration you will face as you begin to design patterns.

Fig. D – Do not close off the white areas completely or the design will fall apart on the saw.

WHAT TO LOOK FOR: COMPUTER SOFTWARE

✔ Look for a program that can manipulate photographs. You want to be able to enlarge or reduce a photo to suit your needs.

✔ You want to be able to lighten or darken the photograph with contrast and brightness settings. This is important to the silhouetting process.

✔ You want to be able to turn a color photograph into a black-and-white photograph, commonly called grayscale.

✔ You need to be able to crop the photo to cut out unwanted background elements.

✔ You may want a program that will allow you to piece together elements from many photos.

Special Considerations

Sometimes, the most interesting photo will make the worst pattern. If you can't retake the photo, apply these tricks to create a workable pattern.

Heavy Shadows

I took a picture of my friend's dog, planning to convert the photo to a pattern. Once the film had been developed and I converted the photo, I realized that the shadows were too heavy on one side of the photo to make a workable pattern. Too much of the detail was missing in this area. (Figure A)

The most obvious solution would be to take another photo. Unfortunately, pets don't pose very well, and I really liked how the dog's paws were resting on the arm of a chair. I could draw in the missing information, but as I mentioned before, I am not an artist. For me, the easiest solution in this case was to duplicate the photo and piece the parts together to make a workable pattern.

To do this without the aid of a computer, I make a second picture of the animal and cut out the background with scissors. Then make a few copies of the picture in different brightness levels and sizes until you come up with the beginnings of a workable pattern. I draw a line down the middle of the pattern to separate the good half from the bad half and cut the pattern in two.

Taking the better half, make another copy at the same size and print it out. Turn this copy over, and trace the entire outline of the pattern. This reverses all the lines. Then cut the reversed copy in half and tape the reversed copy and the original copy together. Touch up the pattern with white correction fluid and a black marker. Make a master copy and a second copy to be used as a cut-out pattern.

This process is simpler with the help of a computer. Delete the background and split the picture in the middle. Duplicate the good side, "flop" the new half and match the two halves to make one complete pattern.

This method will also work well for rebuilding an arm or a hand or any other detail missing due to heavy shadows. Instead of taking another photo, first try to duplicate the photo, reverse it and add in the missing part. Use your imagination to work smart and save yourself some time and effort.

Identifying Marks

This method of duplicating parts of the photos works well for people and pets, unless the subject has a major difference between his left and right sides. For example, a photograph of a woman whose hair is parted on the left would not work well.

If the person or pet has an identifying mark on one side, you can simply draw it in. These small marks are what people are looking for in a picture of their child or pet. Try to include them whenever possible. You don't need to be an artist to add identifying marks.

Figure A – The right side of this photo is too heavily shadowed.

Figure B – Copy the good half of the image and reverse it on a computer or by tracing it from the back.

Figure C – Tape the two halves together to make a workable pattern.

Making a Pattern From a Photograph

Step 1: Basic

I took this candid picture of my son with a single lens reflex, 35mm camera in our backyard. Notice that it has all the qualities of a good pattern-making photo: sharp focus, bright highlights, nice shadows, and an easy-to-remove background.

Step 2: Basic

Here is the same picture converted to black and white. I used a flat-bed scanner to scan it into my computer. You can choose to convert a color photo to black-and-white as you scan it, or scan the photo into the computer in color and then convert it to black-and-white in a photo-manipulation program.

Step 3: Basic

In this case, I'll need to remove the background of the photo before I make my silhouette. Use the tools in the photo-manipulation program to erase the background.

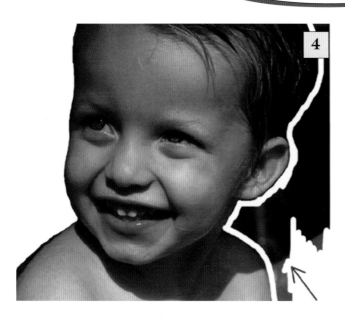

Step 4: Basic

The background on the left side of the photo has been removed. I am now working on erasing the background on the opposite side of the photo. It is not necessary to be exact, but try to be as accurate as possible.

Step 5: Basic

Notice that I left a little bit of the background showing around the lighter parts of the skin. This will give me an outline and prevent the light areas of the subject from bleeding into the white background when I adjust the brightness and contrast levels.

After step 5 you have some options on how to proceed with your conversion from a picture image to a pattern, depending upon the capabilities of your graphics program. First, you can use an effect or filter to enhance the features of the subject in the picture before you adjust the contrast and brightness settings. Second, you can use a layering technique after you have first adjusted the contrast and brightness settings on your picture. If you are unable to use layering or filters in the program that you own, you can just stick with brightness and contrast settings to get the picture to a point that is workable into a pattern of the subject.

The additional technique of applying filters or of layering maximizes the amount of detail that the pattern will have at the end of the pattern-conversion process. I personally use two different programs because no one program has the right tools to do all of the jobs I require in my pattern-making process. I use one program to capture the image from a scanner and to erase the background, and I use another to add a "poster edges" effect. I move the picture from one program to another to take advantage of the different tools each has to offer.

We will start with the steps for a basic conversion and follow up with two new techniques for adding detail and increasing efficiency in your pattern development.

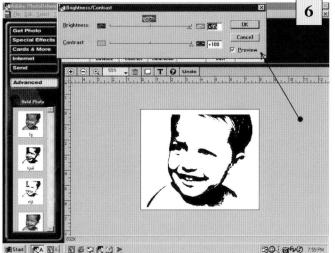

Step 6: Basic

This photo shows a basic contrast and brightness level setting that gets the picture close to a workable pattern. I made this image directly off of the picture in step 5. No effect or filter was added—only the contrast and brightness settings as shown here. Experiment with the contrast and brightness settings at this stage to manipulate the subject's image so that you have the most detail for making your pattern. If the image is too dark, some details will be missing or blacked out. If the image is too bright, the white will wash out some of the darker details.

Step 7: Basic

Now comes the fun part. Keep in mind that the black areas will be cut away on the scroll saw, leaving only the white areas. Those white areas need to be connected and not cut off from one another, or the design will fall apart on the scroll saw. Here are some techniques I use to make the pattern work.

    1) Smooth out rough lines.
    2) Color in isolated white areas, such as this shadow above the eyelid.
    3) Isolate small black areas, such as this shadow under the eye. Eyes are difficult. I add in little peaks to help define where the eye is positioned. The viewer's mind's eye fills in the rest.
    4) Support the face piece by erasing some of the black.

Step 8: Basic

Note all the thin black lines and isolated white spots in this area of the hair. Some changes need to be made here to make this a workable pattern.

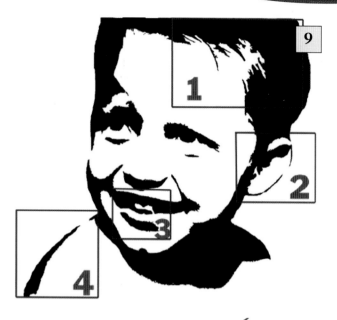

Step 9: Basic

1) This area shows the reworked hair from the previous photo.
2) I erased some of the black line around the ear so that the white areas are not separated from each other.
3) I erased some of the black under the right tooth to connect the white of the teeth to the face.
4) I erased the black that connected the shadow under the lip to the mouth. Isolating this shadow will give the finished piece more strength.

Step 10: Basic

The top of the head was cut off on the original photo. I drew the head shape in freehand and am now filling it in with black.

TIP

Here is a neat way to give the pattern some realism. Try adding simple half-moon ramps to give the illusion of eyes.

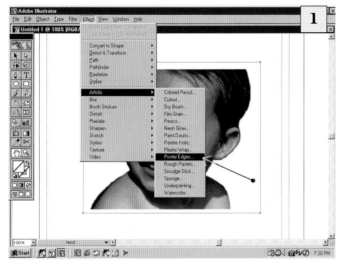

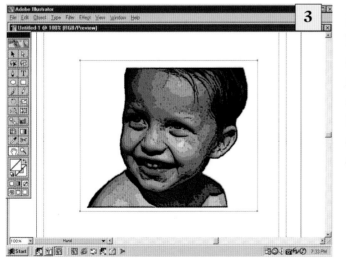

Technique 1: Poster Edges

Step 1: Poster Edges

If your program permits, try out the poster edges effect or filter.

Step 2: Poster Edges

This program (Adobe Illustrator 9.0) has a preview box that shows the adjustments you can make using the slide bars below it. The preview box shows what the image will look like at the bar settings without actually modifying the image.

Step 3: Poster Edges

Notice on this picture that all of the features, such as the ear lines, eye shadows and other prominent character marks are darkened because of the poster edges effect added to the picture. When I now apply a contrast and brightness level to the picture, it will highlight those details that the poster edges has enhanced and made clearer.

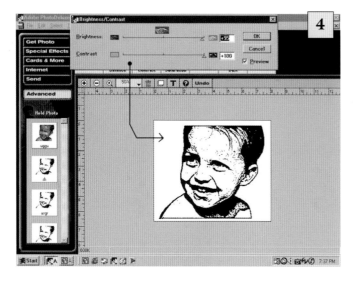

Step 4: Poster Edges

This photo shows the enhanced picture with poster edges and a brightness and contrast setting applied. Notice that the eye shadow and ear detail show through right away. You will have to experiment with your graphics program to achieve proper settings for the contrast and brightness levels. Some programs apply this feature differently, so the result may not look exactly the same as the one shown here.

Step 5: Poster Edges

Both of the examples shown here have the same brightness and contrast levels. You will notice now that the poster edges effect has added detail that would have been missed. After this step, return to touch up and finish—steps 7 to 10 in the basic technique on pages 17 and 18.

Just from photo · With "poster edges" effect added

Technique 2: Layering

Step 1: Layering

This next technique is called "layering." Layering is nothing more than putting one pattern on top of another. You will notice that I have a pattern on the bottom layer that is on the darker side. The layer on top is a brighter level. These are two individual patterns that I have adjusted with the contrast and brightness settings from the original picture. I first opened up the darker pattern on the screen and then imported or pasted the second pattern on top of that one. Be aware that not all programs have a layering feature. Especially if you plan to produce a lot of patterns, layering is a very good feature, and I recommend it to anyone looking for a graphics program.

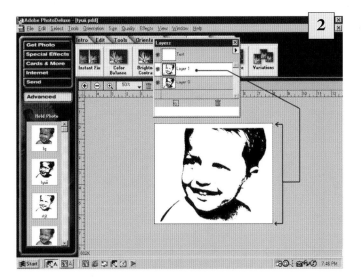

Step 2: Layering

You will notice in this step that I have scaled the top layer to cover the bottom one. Try to line up the edges as best as you can. If you pull or stretch the top layer too far, it will have a different size or dimension than the bottom one. The idea is to have two patterns of the same size layered, one on top of the other.

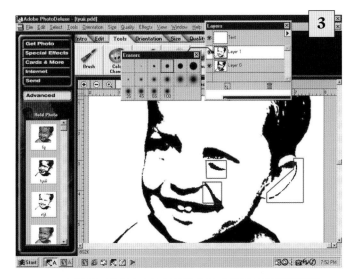

Step 3: Layering

Here is where the magic of layering is revealed. Notice the outlined details in blue. I have chosen an eraser tool to erase small sections of the top pattern to reveal the details in the bottom pattern. Compare the image here with the subject pattern pictured in the previous step. You will notice that the bottom layer detail of the ear, cheek line and eye shadow are now visible. You can work on different areas of the subject in this manner to bring out more detail. If your graphics program does not have a layering feature, you can always print out the two different patterns on your printer and layer the pages. Put them over a light box and trace the detail from the bottom page onto the top page.

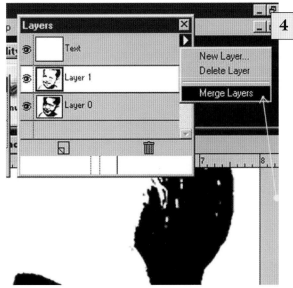

Step 4: Layering

When you are finished with the layering process, you will need to merge the layers together, so that they are just one image instead of two images layered. This program allows me to merge the layers into one as shown. You may have to go through your menu commands to find this merge feature, but you must complete this step in order to move on to the next phase of touching up the pattern.

After this step, return to touch up and finish—steps 7 to 10 in the basic technique on pages 17 and 18.

The pattern is now complete. Look carefully and you'll see that none of the white areas are completely cut off. Remember, the white area is the wood and the black areas will be cut away.

PORTRAIT TECHNIQUES

An Overview of Tools

If you plan to purchase a scroll saw, there are many choices. The best advice I can give you is to purchase the best one you can afford. If you plan to do a lot of scrolling you will find out later that you may need those few extra inches of throat clearance or that quick blade change. Make sure your new saw has a quick blade replacement feature. Wrenches and screw drivers will eventually frustrate you to no end. Avoid saws that take only the blades with the T-holds on the ends. These require a large pilot hole. Look for a way to adjust blade tension and at least two speed settings. Handy accessories such as a foot controlled on–off switch, saw stand, and magnifying lamp can be added later on.

Ask your friends who scroll or look on the internet for scroll saw bulletin boards, clubs or websites. There is a wealth of information on the internet. Learning from other people's mistakes will put you ahead of the game. Scrollers will also give you invaluable tips and tell you if something has not worked for them.

Wood Selection

Wood selection is an important issue. Scrollers today are faced with a wide variety of project wood and other scrolling materials. When choosing wood, keep in mind that solid woods have short grains and will become very fragile on cuts that are very thin.

I prefer ⅛-inch or ¼-inch birch or oak plywood. This type of plywood can be easily found at your local home improvement store or lumber yard. It fits very nicely into a standard glass-covered picture frame. Well-treated wood will not require any staining or painting, and the

A spiral blade allows you to cut in any direction.

light color of the wood stands out well against the black backgrounds.

PART TWO

Blade Selection

Blade selection is another important issue. I use a spiral blade on all my work. I find this type of blade allows me to move the wood smoothly along the sometimes intricate lines of a portrait pattern. It also moves extremely fast, cutting down on the amount of time needed to scroll a piece.

If you are not familiar with using a spiral blade, be sure to practice first on a piece of scrap wood. Its operation is quite different than a traditional blade, and you may need some practice time before you become comfortable using it. Try moving the wood backwards, forwards, left and right while cutting. Try not to rotate the wood clockwise or counter-clockwise. Practice this exercise until you feel comfortable with the feel of the blade.

Additional Considerations

Remove burrs from the back of the work with a knife.

Burrs: A spiral blade is fast, but it leaves additional work to be done on the back side of the piece. You will find that there are a number of burrs that need to be removed before the piece can be mounted. A small engraving tool with a little round diamond tipped ball removes burrs quickly and easily. A utility or carving knife can also be used to remove burrs, but be careful that you don't slice away too much wood with the sharp blade. Sandpaper is an inexpensive method, but also the most time-consuming method.

Black Backgrounds: I always use black felt for the background of my scroll-sawed portraits. You may also want to try using a piece of wood that you have painted black. Different types of material will give your finished portrait a different look. Try silk for a more modern feel or burlap for a "country" feel. You may also want to experiment with colors other than black. An application of glue from a hot glue gun will help keep the background material firmly in place.

Frames: Frame your project to give it the appearance of a beautiful painted silhouette. Admirers of your work will be pleasantly surprised to find out that quite a bit of workmanship went in to creating your "painting." The glass will also help to protect the wood from nicks and scratches and keep dust from settling on the black background.

If you are ambitious, you can make your own frames. I buy mine at a discount store. I find I enjoy scrolling portraits more than cutting frames, and purchasing the frames gives me more time to enjoy my hobby. Purchased frames also come complete with matting, glass and backing material.

Computers: The computer is a useful tool for completing many tasks. Scrolling is no different. I use a computer, scanner and printer to generate my patterns. If you do not own a computer, check with your local library or school. Oftentimes, time can be scheduled on their equipment. Portrait patterns can also be created the traditional way, with tracing paper and a pencil. (See the pattern-making techniques in Part One.)

Pattern Transfer: If you are using a computer to create your pattern, simply use the standard white copy paper that fits most printers. As you learn more about scrolling portraits and designing patterns, you may want to try printing your pattern to iron-on transfer paper, acetate sheets, or heavy-weight paper. Traditional artists will want to use tracing paper to create their patterns, then transfer the final drawing to a clean sheet of paper or other media.

Mounting the Pattern

You can mount the pattern to the plywood several ways. As you work with portrait patterns, try these different methods. All of them work equally well; your choice should be based on personal preference.

One of the fastest ways to mount a pattern is to use a spray can of temporary adhesive. Spray the back of the pattern—not the wood—so the pattern can be easily removed. Spraying both the pattern and the wood or just the wood will often cause the paper to become too sticky and make it difficult to remove.

Another way to transfer a pattern is to use carbon or graphite paper. Place a piece of carbon paper between the pattern and the wood, black or blue side down. Tape the edges of the pattern and the carbon paper securely to the wood. Trace around the black areas of the pattern with a pencil, ball point pen or stylus. As you trace, the pattern outline will be transferred to the wood.

You can also print the pattern out on a full sheet of sticker paper or self-adhesive paper. Then simply peel off the back of the paper and stick it to the wood. Some online companies have this type of paper that is made to their specifications and works very well. Many office supply stores also carry their version for making stickers from your computer.

A good practice is to cover the top of the pattern with clear packaging tape, regardless of what method you use to mount the pattern. You can also cover the wood with painter's tape, and then use temporary bond spray adhesive on the back of the pattern and on the top of the painter's tape. Apply the pattern directly after spraying, so that it sticks to the painter's tape with a good strong bond. Once the piece is cut, the painter's tape and pattern both peel right off with little or no residue. Painter's tape is typically blue in color. It can be expensive to continually use, but it is very reliable. Both painter's tape and packaging tape help to lubricate the blade, so that it cuts better and holds up longer.

Stack Cutting

Try cutting two or three pieces of wood at the same time to yield multiple copies of the same design. Stack the pieces evenly and secure them with small brads in the corners. A staple gun will also work well. Stack cutting will cut down dramatically on the amount of time you spend cutting multiple pieces. If it takes you two hours to cut out one project, then the additional pieces will cut your time per piece in half if you stack two pieces of wood and by two-thirds if you stack three pieces of wood. Stack cutting also increases your chances that one of the pieces will be completed without blemishes.

Fixing Mistakes

One of the most frustrating things that can happen as you work on a scrollsawed portrait is to make a mistake on a piece that you are trying your best to do perfectly. It is inevitable that you will make mistakes. There are, however, ways to avoid mistakes and ways to fix the mistakes you make.

You can avoid most mistakes completely by following some common sense rules. 1) Do not stress over the little mistakes. This is a very relaxing hobby, unless you let the little things get to you. 2) Take your time as you start a project. Cut slowly until you get that feeling of confidence that will allow you to increase your speed. 3) Scroll only when you are well rested and can keep your mind on your work.

For those mistakes that do happen, don't despair. There's no need to scrap the whole project if you break a few fragile pieces. There is a good reason why scientists invented glue. When a piece breaks off, remember where the piece goes and set it aside. Put a

little spot of wood glue on the piece when you are done cutting and carefully glue it back in place. Once the clear coat is on the final piece and your project is behind glass, the mistake will be invisible.

Most of the mistakes made when scrolling portraits happen on the small, tight cuts that have a lot of ins and outs. These small mistakes are really no big deal because the patterns you use are your own creations, made from photographs. No one will have any idea you made a mistake unless you take out the original photograph and point out the mistake.

Transfer the Pattern

Fig. A

Fig. B

1 Study the pattern carefully before you begin. As soon as the first piece of wood is cut out, the whole piece of wood is not as strong as it was originally. Many times, there are a lot of thin pieces of cut wood that have to support a larger piece. To give the wood more stability, you should start somewhere in the middle of the wood and work your way toward the outer cuts. Mark your pattern or the wood to show the order of the cuts. In this demonstration, the cuts shown above in blue will be completed first; the cuts shown in red will be done last.

2 Use carbon paper to transfer the pattern to the wood. I am working on an 8 ½ x 11 piece of birch plywood that is ¼-inch thick.

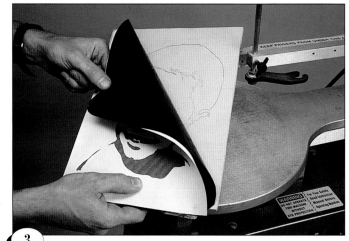

3 Check that you've traced all the lines by lifting the corners of the carbon paper.

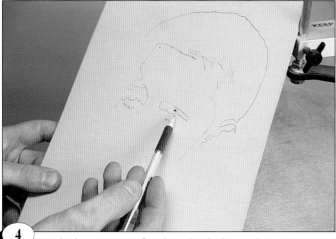

4 Mark the positions for the pilot holes as shown in Step 1.

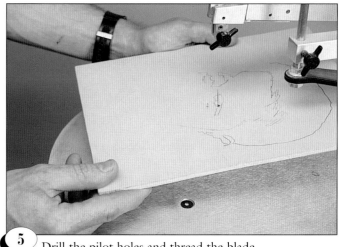

5 Drill the pilot holes and thread the blade.

Making the Inside Cuts

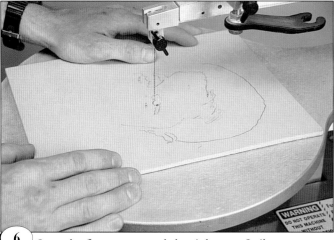

6 Start the first cut around the right eye. Strike a comfortable stance and apply slight pressure to the board.

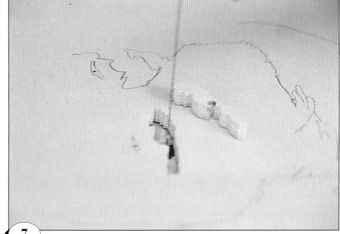

7 Cut completely around the eye in one smooth motion. As you finish the cut, power down the saw and carefully remove the waste wood.

Making the Outside Cuts

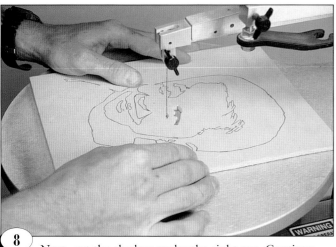

8 Next, cut the shadow under the right eye. Continue cutting until you've finished all of the inside cuts.

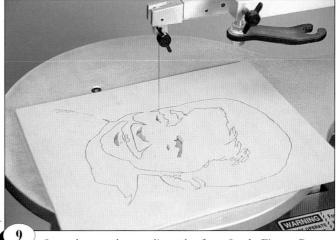

9 Start the cut that outlines the face. Study Figure B at the beginning of this demonstration. Notice that the red area is removed with one long cut.

SCROLL SAW PORTRAITS

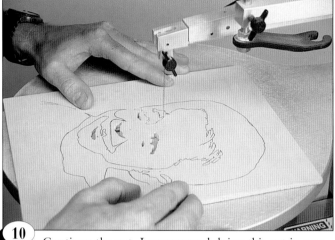

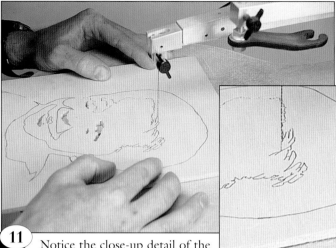

10 Continue the cut. I recommend doing this cut in one motion because it is hard to pick up where you left off when using a spiral blade.

11 Notice the close-up detail of the hairline on the forehead.

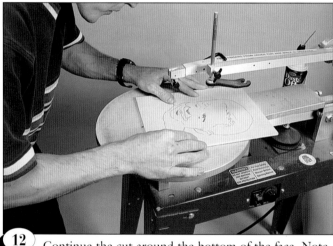

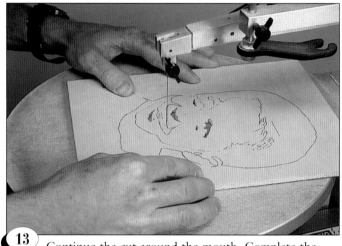

12 Continue the cut around the bottom of the face. Note that both hands are in contact with the wood and the table at all times. Both hands are needed to steady and guide the wood.

13 Continue the cut around the mouth. Complete the rest of the outside cuts.

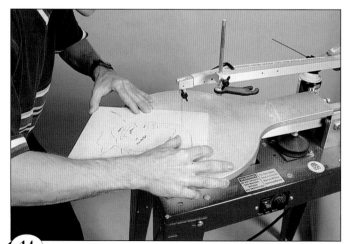

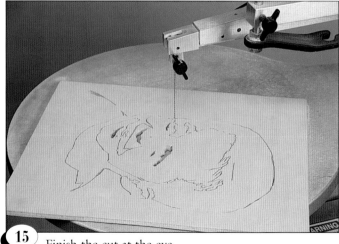

14 The long outside cut is almost done. Note the stance. It is important to stay relaxed, especially when making long cuts such as this one.

15 Finish the cut at the eye.

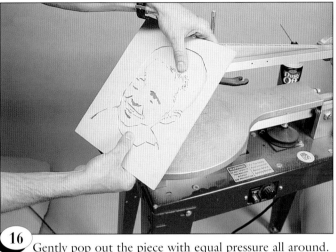

16 Gently pop out the piece with equal pressure all around.

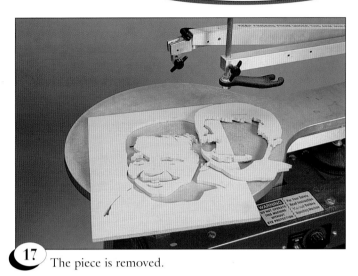

17 The piece is removed.

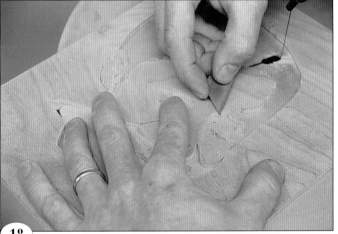

18 Turn the project over and remove the burrs from the back of the wood.

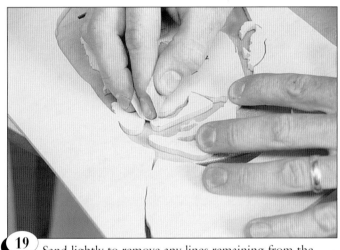

19 Sand lightly to remove any lines remaining from the pattern transfer. Apply several coats of a clear spray finish.

Mount the Project

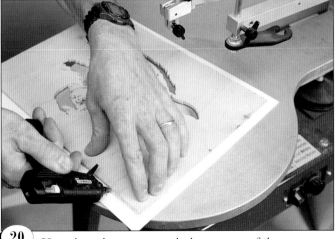

20 Use a hot glue gun to tack the corners of the mat to the project.

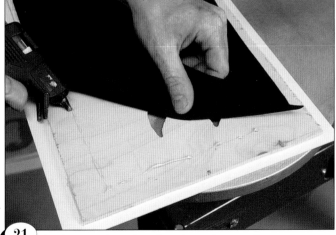

21 Apply more hot glue directly to the wood.

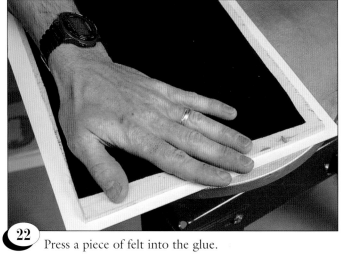

22 Press a piece of felt into the glue.

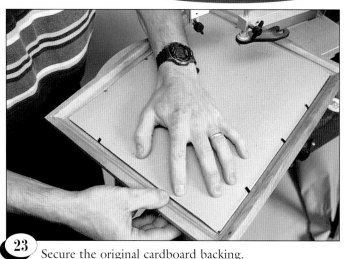

23 Secure the original cardboard backing.

The finished piece is ready for display.

CREATIVE
USES

Many people have e-mailed me and spoken to me about some very creative ideas to try. Sometimes, there is a particular photograph or person they think would make a good subject for a scrolled portrait. Other times, they have ideas on how to use the patterns differently. I file all these ideas away in the back of my head. Even the ideas that sound a little off the wall may help me with a future project.

Following are some ideas that I have developed. They take portrait scrolling one step further. I hope that they may aid you in some way, or at least get you thinking about some new ideas of your own.

Decorative paints

Use some of the specialty paints found in home improvement stores to give your finished piece a different look. Some paints will give the wood the look of stone or metal.

Stencils

Create patterns for your home or business and then cut them to use as stencils. Many companies have difficulty finding graphics as well. Making a stencil from their logo or from a unique photo relating to their company is an inexpensive way to help a business build a company identity. The stencils can be used to make signs or label company cars.

To make a stencil from a pattern, simply sandwich a

Decorative specialty paint gives this wooden portrait of a butterfly the look of stone.

piece of posterboard or clear plastic between two pieces of wood. Secure the materials with staples along the edges of the wood or place brads in the corners. Transfer the pattern to the wood and cut the project. When you are finished you'll have two wooden cuttings of the pattern and one heavy-duty stencil.

You can also make stencils without scrolling two pieces of wood as well. Simply trace the pattern onto thick posterboard or use graphite paper to transfer it to clear plastic. Use a utility knife or hobby knife to cut out the areas that you would normally remove with the scroll saw.

Stencils can also be used to brighten up your home. Use them with regular paints or sponge paints to decorate a wall or a door. I like to use stencils to apply a paint called frosting to glass. I made an eagle pattern into a stencil for a friend of mine and used it to spray a frosted eagle on the back window of his truck. The result was the appearance of etched glass.

Frosting also works well to apply designs to your windows during holiday seasons. Frosted angels and evergreen trees look great on windows at Christmas time. You can also use stencils and frosting to add a border to glass mirrors. Best of all, unlike real glass etchings, the frosted paint can be removed easily with a razor blade.

Coloring Books

The patterns you create double as instant coloring pages. Just trace the outline of a pattern and photocopy the pages to make a coloring book for a special child. If you are using a computer to make patterns, the patterns are easily converted to outlines using an illustration or photo manipulation program. Imagine how tickled a youngster would be to receive a coloring book with pictures of mom, dad and all his favorite people.

Sun Catchers

Instead of framing your finished project, try adding some colored plastic or glass to the back. This will make a beautiful sun catcher for your window and really sets off pieces like bird houses and small frames.

Greeting Cards

Try making your own greeting cards with the patterns you develop for the scroll saw. A number of sheets of heavier weight paper can be sandwiched tightly between two pieces of wood. Cut out the pattern, remove the paper and fold to create a card. Add a backing of a different color to the front of the card and you have a beautiful finished project to give to friends on birthdays, holidays and other special occasions.

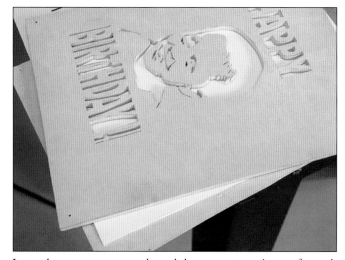

Insert heavy paper or card stock between two pieces of wood and cut the pattern.

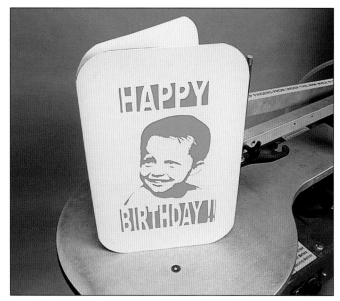

The author created this card on the scroll saw for his son's birthday.

Veneer

One final idea is to decorate wooden cabinets and doors with veneer cut-outs made on your scroll saw. Veneer, which is very thin, laminated strips of wood, can be purchased at home improvement stores. Look for the new rolls of veneer that have a sticky backing.

Sandwich this backing between two pieces of wood and cut out a pattern. The veneer pattern can then be ironed on to cabinets, doors or other wooden objects. Imagine creating a small bread box or chest that has a loved one's reflection. These are gifts that will be treasured and passed down to the next generation.

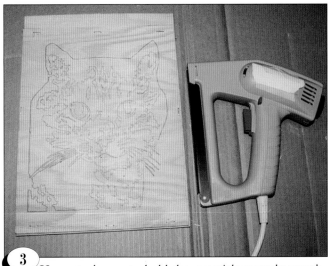

1 Sticky-backed iron-on veneer can be bought in rolls at home improvement stores.

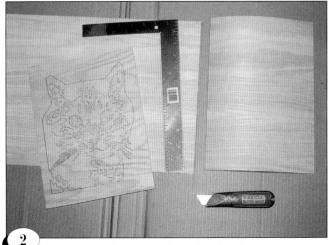

2 Cut a piece of veneer and sandwich it between two pieces of plywood.

3 Use a staple gun to hold the materials securely together as you cut.

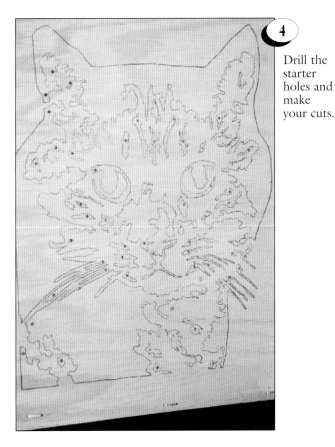

4 Drill the starter holes and make your cuts.

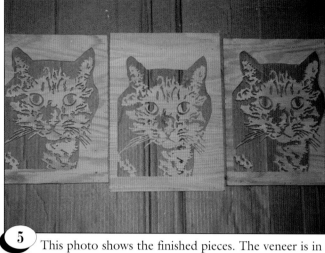

5 This photo shows the finished pieces. The veneer is in the center.

6 Tape the veneer to a cabinet or other wooden object.

7 Use a hot iron to activate the sticky backing on the veneer. Iron the center first, remove the tape, then iron the rest.

The veneer cat mounted on a white cabinet door.

A small area of the cabinet door was painted black on this version. You can frame this piece with trim for a "built-in" look.

PORTRAIT PATTERNS

The main goal of this book is to show you how to create your own portrait patterns from photos that you have taken. But if you are like me, you will want to jump right in and prove to yourself that you can actually create beautiful portraits.

Most of these patterns have been cut out by me, and after cutting out many of them, I know from experience that every pattern in this book is a workable pattern. I have spent a lot of time preparing the patterns to make them available to you without any more effort than copying, mounting and cutting them out.

If you feel that an area of the pattern will be too fragile for you to cut, modify it to meet your ability. Many of these patterns may seem difficult unless you have had some previous saw time. If you are a beginner, you may want to start with these patterns until you are comfortable with the feel of the blade and the saw. Note: The patterns in this section were generated by a computer, as evidenced by the slightly jagged outlines. I use carbon paper to transfer the patterns and smooth out the lines as I trace.

I hope that by finishing just one of these patterns that you will feel as I did in the beginning: creative, inspired and ready for more!

A NOTE ABOUT COPYRIGHT

Copyright can be a very difficult legal area to understand. Basically, copyright (©) protects the owner from unwanted copying and loss of income. When making your own patterns, be sure to use copyright-free images, such as photos or illustrations you have made yourself or public domain material. For more information on copyright issues, check your local library or do an Internet search under copyright.

Cat

Cat

Cat

Cat

Horse

Stallion

Dog

Cute puppy

Greyhound

Dog

Husky

German Shepherd

Roaring lion

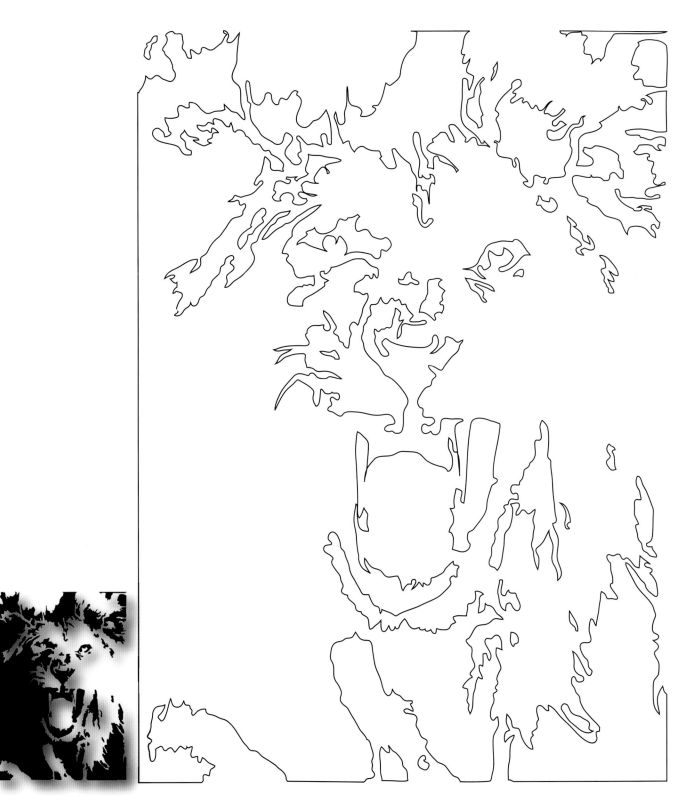

Roaring lion

Leopard

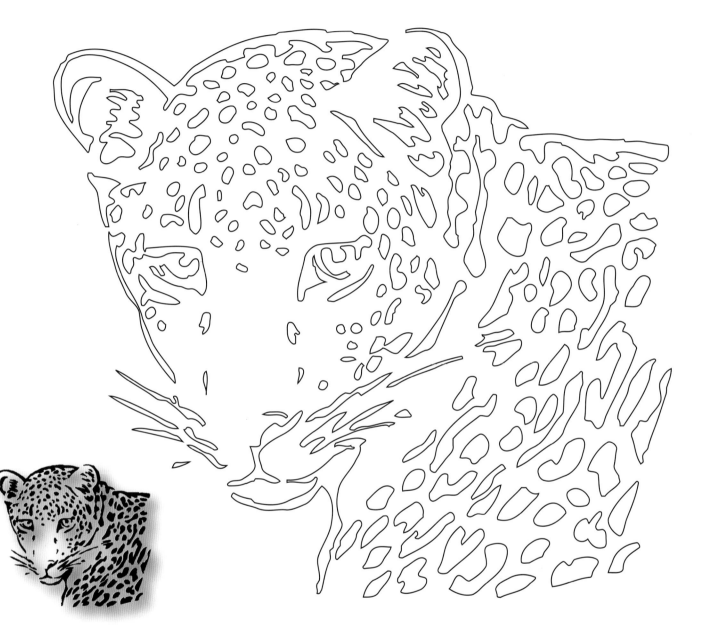

Leopard

Buck

Buck

Ram

Bear eating salmon

Polar Bear

WILD ANIMALS

Howling Wolf

SCROLL SAW PORTRAITS

57

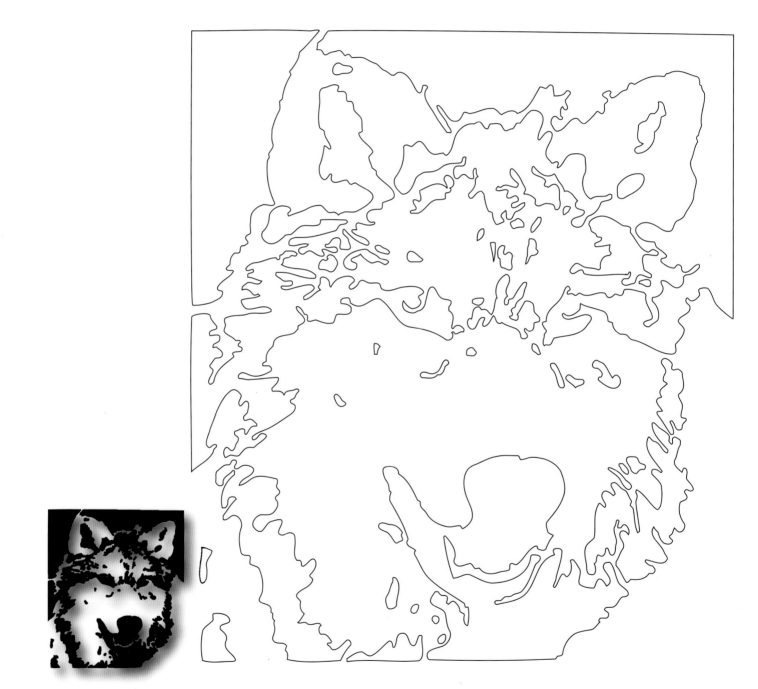

Wolf

Camel

Rhino

Chimpanzee

Koala

Owl

Bald Eagle

Bald Eagle

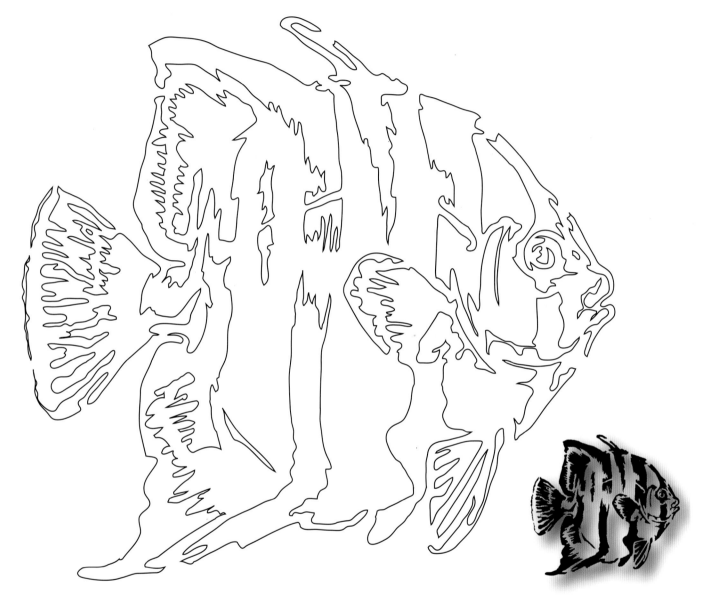

Angel Fish

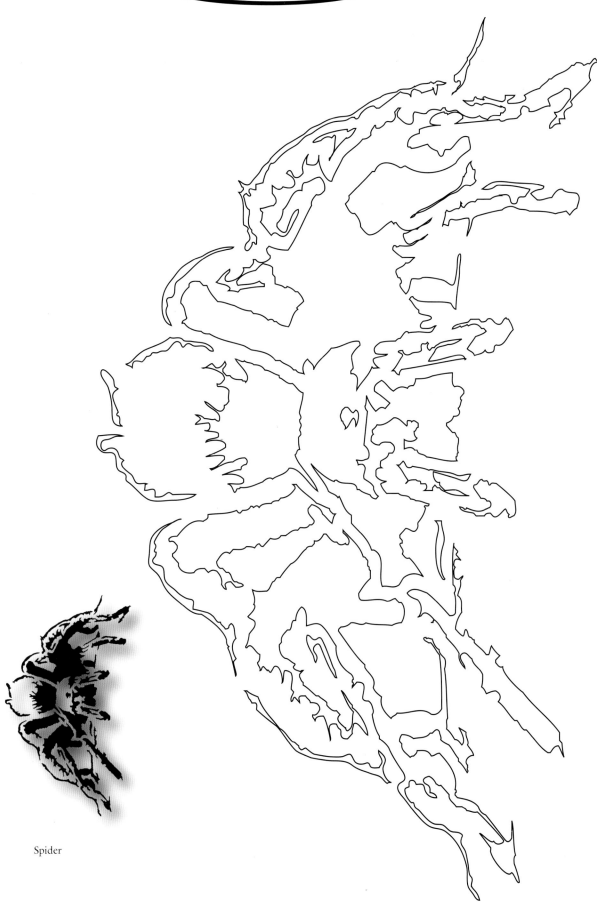

Spider

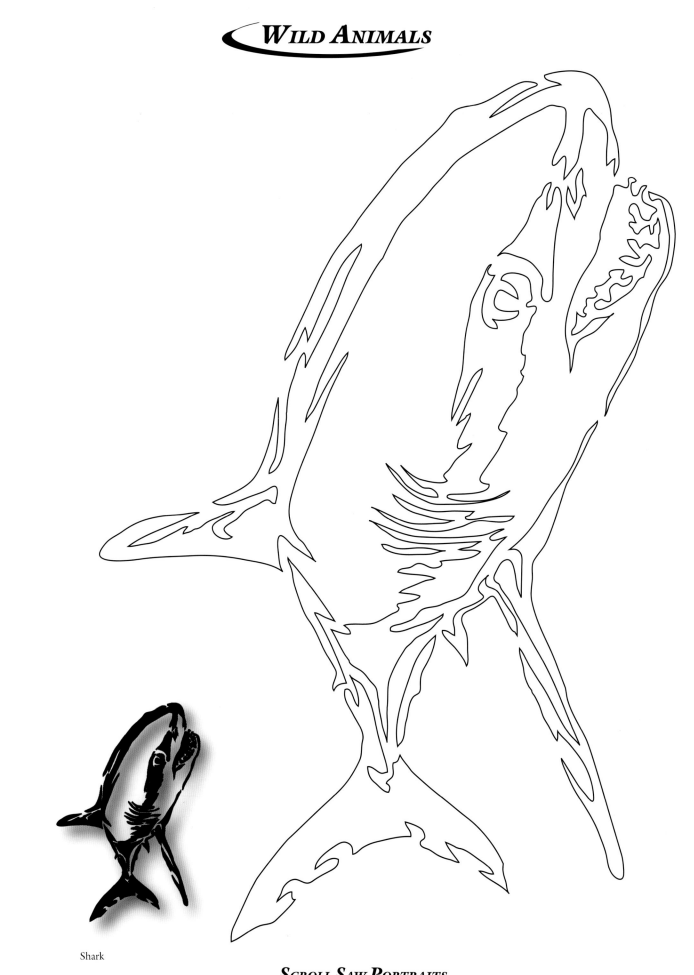

Shark

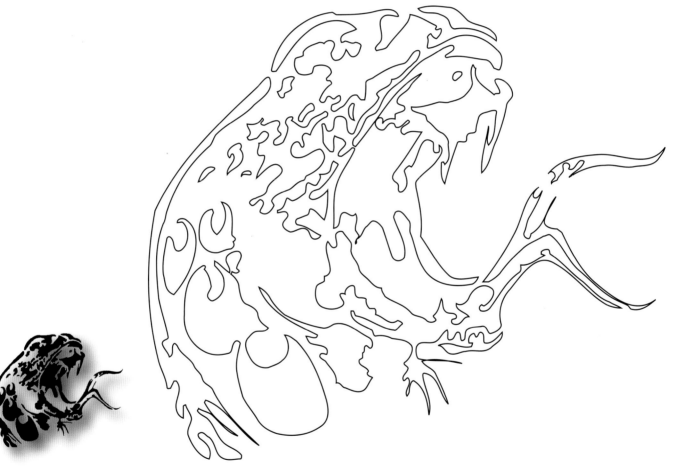

Snake

Frog

Seahorse

Jesus

Jesus

Mary

Mary

Mary with Jesus

Pope John Paul

Angel

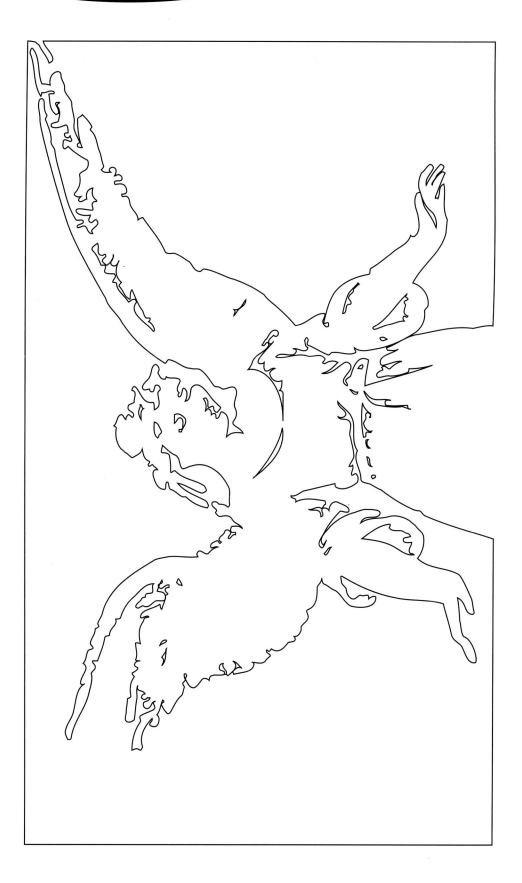

Guardian Angel

Curley, Custer's Indian Scout,
only survivor of Custer's Last Stand

Chief

Medicine Man

Native American

Native American Mother and Child

Cowboy

Robert E. Lee

Ulysses S. Grant

Abraham Lincoln

Ronald Reagan

War Hero

Marines

Raising the Flag

Marine

Albert Einstein

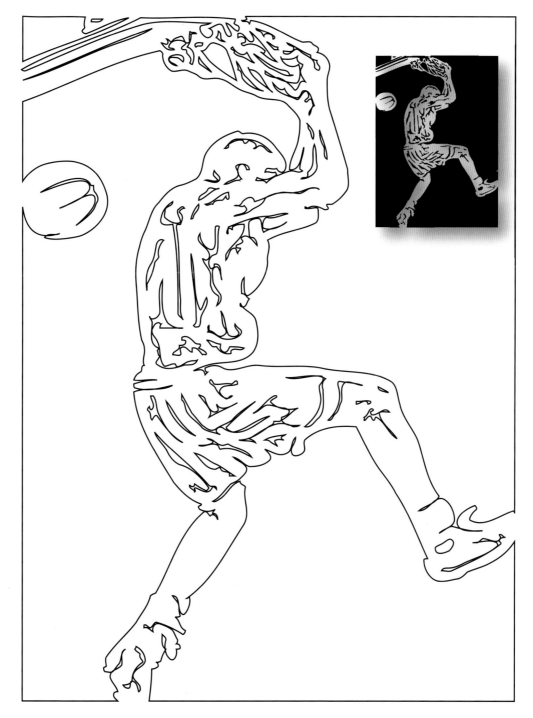

Basketball

Soccer

Skateboarding

Skiing

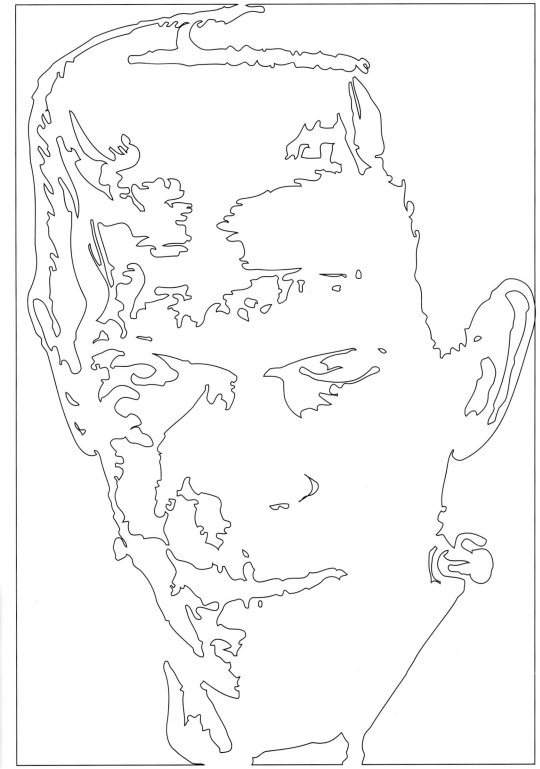

Frankenstein

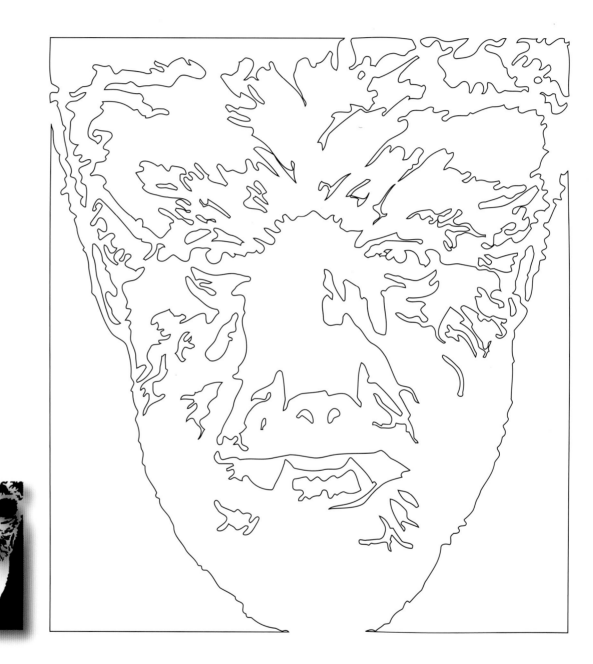

Wolfman

Frank Sinatra

John Wayne

Humphrey Bogart

W.C. Fields

Gene Autrey

Groucho Marx